Presented to:

_____

From:

_____

Psalm 127:3

ZONDERVAN®

You're the Best Mom!

Copyright © 2014 by Zondervan

Requests for information should be addressed to:

Zondervan, Grand Rapids, Michigan 49530

ISBN 978-0-310-33991-5

Cover design: Milkglass Creative, LLC
Cover illustration: Milkglass Creative, LLC
Interior design: Mallory Perkins
Stock images p 10, 11, 26, 27, 40, 56/miumiu © Shutterstock
Printed in the United States of America

14 15 16 17 18 19 20 21 /Taylor/ 10 9 8 7 6 5 4 3 2

YOU'RE

— THE —

Best

MOM!

TABLE OF CONTENTS

Whatever is true, whatever is noble, whatever is right, whatever is pure, whatever is lovely, whatever is admirable—if anything is excellent or praiseworthy—think about such things.
—Philippians 4:8

Her favorite TV show was

_____.

Her favorite food was

_____.

The chore she hated most was

_____.

Her favorite hobby was

_____.

Mom had a pet that was a:

a. dog   c. fish
b. cat   d. rock

MOM'S FAVORITES

Mom's favorite color is

_____.

Mom's favorite song is

_____.

Mom's favorite food is

_____.

Mom's favorite restaurant is

_____.

Mom's favorite game to play is

_____.

MOM AT WORK

What kind of job does Mom have?

_____

What does Mom do when she is at work?

_____

If you went to work with Mom for a day,
how would you help her do her job?

_____

A DAY IN THE LIFE OF MOM

Fill in Mom's calendar with what
she does on a typical day.

What time does Mom . . .

Wake up? _____

Make breakfast? _____

Go to work? _____

Eat lunch? _____

Pick me up from school? _____

Run errands? _____

Go to bed? _____

MOM ESSENTIALS

What is Mom's name?

_____

How old is Mom?

_____

How tall is Mom?

_____

How much does Mom weigh?

_____

What color are Mom's eyes?

_____

What color is Mom's hair?

_____

Draw a picture of what Mom looks like!

Do you and Mom share any interests?
Check all of the things you both enjoy!

- [ ] reading books
- [ ] singing
- [ ] playing outside
- [ ] cooking
- [ ] watching movies
- [ ] shopping

MOM AS A SUPERHERO

If your mom really did have a superpower, what would it be?

_____

Who would her sidekick be?

_____

How would your mom and her sidekick save the world?

_____

_____

_____

_____

_____

Draw a picture of Mom and her
sidekick in their superhero costumes!

Her children arise and call her blessed;
her husband also, and he praises her:
"Many women do noble things,
but you surpass them all."

—PROVERBS 31:28-29

SCHOOL DAYS

What is the name of your school?

_____

What are your favorite subjects in school?

_____

Who is your favorite teacher?

_____

What is in your favorite school lunch?

_____

Tell Mom about your day at school in one word.

_____

Draw a picture of how you get to school!
Do you walk, ride in a car, or take the bus?

PLAYGROUND FUN

What is your favorite thing to do on the playground or at the park?

_____

What do you think Mom would like to do most at the playground or park? Why?

_____

Check all the things your mom can do:

- ☐ Jump higher than a building
- ☐ Catch a ball
- ☐ Climb to the top of the jungle gym
- ☐ Swing higher than the top of the swing set
- ☐ Slide down the slide
- ☐ Win a foot race
- ☐ Jump 100 times over the jump rope without tripping
- ☐ Win a game of tag
- ☐ See-saw with me
- ☐ Swing all the way across the monkey bars

THIS OR THAT?

Circle the one Mom would choose:

TV shows or movies?   Tea or cola?

Chocolate or vanilla?   Dogs or cats?

Sleeping in late or waking up early?

The beach or the mountains?

Spiders or worms?   Cheese or chocolate?

Playing outside or reading a book?

Hamburger or hot dog?   Cook or get takeout?

Fold laundry or wash dishes?

ANIMAL ANTICS

If Mom were an animal, what animal would she be? Why?

_____

What animal would you be? Why?

_____

What is your favorite animal?

_____

What is Mom's favorite animal?

_____

Draw your mom's favorite animal!

IN THE KITCHEN WITH MOM

My favorite dish Mom makes is

_____.

My mom makes the best

_____ in the whole world.

I like it when Mom makes

_____ for breakfast.

I like it when Mom makes

_____ for dinner.

On my birthday I want my mom to make me

_____ as a special treat.

My mom's favorite type of food to cook is

_____.

When Mom orders takeout, we usually have

_____.

OUR FAMILY HOME

Which state do you live in?

_____

What is the name of the town where you live?

_____

What is your favorite room in your house?

_____

What color is your room?

_____

Do you have your own room, or do you share it with someone?

_____

Is your room usually clean, or is it usually pretty messy?

_____

Draw a picture of you and your mom in front of your house!

MOM ON SUNDAY

The name of my church is

_____.

I like to sing this song with Mom:

_____.

Mom usually wears _____ to church.

My mom's favorite Bible story is

_____.

Mom's favorite place to eat after church is

_____.

When it comes to arriving at church, my mom typically:

a. gets to church pretty early
b. arrives right on time for church
c. can be a little late sometimes

Mom is most likely to do which one of these things at church?

a. Sing in the choir
b. Work in the nursery
c. Help with refreshments
d. Teach Sunday school

MOM SAYS . . .

Fill the speech bubbles with things
that Mom says the most.

My favorite thing that Mom says is

_____.

PRETTY AS A PICTURE

Attach your favorite photo of Mom to this page, and draw a picture frame around it.

AT THE MOMENT

	Today	When Mom was my age
How much is a can of soda?	_____	_____
Who is the president?	_____	_____
Who is the biggest pop star?	_____	_____
What is the most popular cartoon on TV?	_____	_____

WHEN I GROW UP . . .

I want to live _____.

I want to go to college at _____.

I want to be a _____.

My first job will pay $ _____ a year.

I will go on vacation to _____.

MOM IS BETTER AT . . .

Do you think your mom would be better
at painting a picture, building a birdhouse,
or running a race? Why?

_____.

_____.

_____.

_____.

_____.

_____.

_____.

_____.

Do you think your mom would be better at . . . (circle one on each line)

a. being a lunch lady

b. being president of the United States

a. being a famous painter

b. being a construction worker

a. cooking a Thanksgiving meal

b. eating a Thanksgiving meal

a. running a science lab

b. running a daycare

a. growing flowers

b. growing rocks

a. being a football player

b. being a baseball player

a. surfing a huge ocean wave

b. snowboarding down a mountain

a. walking on dinosaur feet

b. walking on caterpillar feet

a. milking a cow

b. herding sheep

a. kicking a field goal

b. dancing in The Nutcracker

MY FUNNY MOM

The most embarrassing thing Mom
has ever done to me is

_____.

My mom thinks she is funny when she

_____.

I think Mom is funny when she

_____.

Mom's favorite joke is

_____.

What's the funniest April Fool's joke
Mom has ever played on you?

_____

MOM DOES GREAT THINGS

What is the nicest thing Mom has ever done for you?

_____

What is the kindest thing you've seen
Mom do for someone else?

_____

What is the coolest thing Mom has ever said to you?

_____

Draw a picture of the time your
mom helped you the most!

MOM IS BEAUTIFUL

Help Mom see what she looks like by
drawing the parts of her beautiful face!

Mom's nose looks like this:

Mom's smile looks like this:

Mom's hair looks like this:

Mom's eyes look like this:

Mom's ears look like this:

Do you look like your mom? Check all
of the features you both share!

- ☐ eye color
- ☐ nose shape
- ☐ hair color
- ☐ ear shape
- ☐ smile

PARTY PLANNER

When is Mom's birthday?

_____

What is Mom's favorite present
you've ever given to her?

_____

If you could give Mom anything,
what gift would you give her?

_____

What is Mom's favorite birthday tradition?

_____

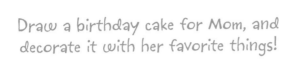

Draw a birthday cake for Mom, and decorate it with her favorite things!

MEDIA MOM

Reading

Mom and I like to read:

a. picture books   c. magazines
b. my Bible   d. Internet websites

Our favorite book is about _____.

When we read my Bible, we like to read about _____.

Music

Mom's favorite type of music is _____.

Her favorite radio station is _____.

Mom's favorite song is _____.

Mom's favorite band is _____.

When Mom dances and sings, I think she is:

a. good
b. really good
c. a real star
d. well . . . she might need a few pointers from me

Shopping

Mom's favorite place to shop is _____.

Mom's favorite thing to buy is_____.

I like shopping with Mom because _____.

My favorite store to go to with Mom is _____

because _____.

TV

Mom's favorite TV show is _____.

If they made a TV show about my mom, she would

be played by _____.

My favorite show to watch with Mom is _____

_____.

MOM ON THE FARM

What are Mom's favorite vegetables?

_____

If Mom were a farmer, which plants would she grow?

_____

If Mom were a farmer, I think she would definitely have:

a. horses   d. sheep
b. chickens   e. pigs
c. cows

If Mom was a farm animal, I think she would be a

_____.

My favorite farm animal is

_____.

If I was a farmer, I would plant

_____.

I think my mom would be a
great farmer because she

_____.

Draw a picture of your
mom dressed like a farmer!

FLOWERS FOR MOM

Mom's favorite flower is

_____.

Draw a bouquet of Mom's favorite flowers!

LESSONS FROM MOM

What is something that Mom is great at doing?

_____

What is your favorite thing that
Mom has taught you to do?

_____

What are three things you want
Mom to teach you to do?

1. _____

2. _____

3. _____

MOM IS MY FAVORITE!

Attach your favorite picture of your mom below. Why is it your favorite?

_____

_____

_____

_____

Attach your favorite picture of you and your mom together below. Why is this picture special to you?

_____

_____

_____

_____

[Love] always protects, always trusts, always hopes, always perseveres.
— 1 Corinthians 13:7

SPECIAL DAYS

VACATION

I think Mom would rather go to:
(circle one on each line)

a. Disney World   b. Paris, France
a. the Grand Canyon   b. the Mall of America
a. Las Vegas   b. Vermont
a. Hawaii   b. Alaska
a. Chuck E. Cheese's   b. McDonald's

When we're on vacation, my mom would like to stay in:

a. a hotel   b. a camping tent

My mom's favorite vacation we've ever taken is

_____.

My mom's favorite thing do to on vacation is

_____.

On vacation, my mom would rather:

a. kick back and relax   b. plan tons of activities
                             for us to do

Sometimes, Mom and I go out by ourselves. I

like it when we go to _____.

If I had the whole day to spend with Mom, I

would want us to _____.

The best day I ever spent with Mom was when we

_____

_____

_____.

FANCY FUN

Have you and Mom ever been to a:

- ☐ birthday party
- ☐ wedding
- ☐ Christmas party

Do you ever have to dress up for special days?

_____

If you could take your mom somewhere
fancy, where would you take her? Why?

_____

_____

_____

_____

_____

Draw what Mom looks like when she dresses up!

OUT AND ABOUT

My mom and I like to:

- ☐ go to the movies
- ☐ go shopping at the mall
- ☐ go to the library

If my mom had a day to herself, I think she would go to _____.

When I'm in school, I secretly think my mom goes to _____.

When Mom takes me shopping, I'm:

a. super excited
b. so bored
c. hoping we can get to the toy aisle!

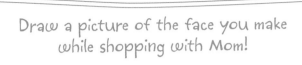

Draw a picture of the face you make
while shopping with Mom!

HAPPY HOLIDAYS

Mom's favorite holiday is

_____.

She likes it because

_____.

My favorite thing about spending holidays with Mom is

_____.

My favorite holiday tradition with Mom is when we

_____.

Mom's favorite holiday tradition is when we

_____.

The best present my mom ever
gave me for a holiday was

_____.

The worst present my mom ever
gave me for a holiday was

_____.

The best present I ever gave my
mom for a holiday was

_____.

I like it when Mom decorates the house for

_____ because

_____.

My favorite holiday meal that Mom makes is

_____.

CHRISTMAS CHEER!

My mom's favorite Christmas song is

_____.

My favorite Christmas ornament is

_____.

My favorite Christmas song is

_____.

My favorite Christmas treat is

_____.

The best Christmas memory I
have with Mom is when

_____.

My mom's favorite Christmas movie is

_____.

My favorite Christmas movie is

_____.

Attach or draw your favorite picture of
you and your mom at the holidays.

BIRTHDAY FACES

Attach a photo of your mom below from one of her birthday parties. On the next page, attach a picture of yourself from your birthday party at the same age. What similarities and differences do you see in the pictures?

Honor your father and your mother, as the LORD your God has commanded you . . .
—Deuteronomy 5:16

ABOUT THE AUTHOR

NAME

_____

AGE

_____

DATE

_____

Mom, I think you are the best because

_____